The Middle Years

PAUL E. JOHNSON

Fortress Press   Philadelphia

POCKET COUNSEL BOOKS

Am I Losing My Faith? by William E. Hulme

Drinking Problem? by John E. Keller

When Marriage Ends by Russell J. Becker

When Someone Dies by Edgar N. Jackson

The Middle Years by Paul E. Johnson

Crisis and Growth: Helping Your Troubled Child
by Charlotte H. and Howard J. Clinebell

ACKNOWLEDGMENT

I acknowledge with profound gratitude the personal communications of many friends, who have shared with me crucial experiences from their own middle life. To them we are indebted for authentic glimpses of what it means to be in the exciting middle of life.

COPYRIGHT © 1971 BY FORTRESS PRESS

All rights reserved. No part of this publication may be reproduced, stored in a retrieval system, or transmitted in any form or by any means, electronic, mechanical, photocopying, recording, or otherwise, without the prior permission of the copyright owner.

Library of Congress Catalog Card Number 70–154489

ISBN 0–8006–1105–5

1835 A71   Printed in the United States of America   1-1105

Series Introduction

Pocket Counsel Books are intended to help people with problems in a specific way. Problems may arise in connection with family life, marriage, grief, alcoholism, drugs or death. In addressing themselves to these and similar problems, the authors have made every effort to speak in language free from technical vocabulary.

Because these books are not only nontechnical but also brief, they offer a good start in helping people with specific problems. Face-to-face conversation between counselor and counselee is a necessary part of the help the authors envision through these books. The books are not a substitute for person-to-person counseling: they supplement counseling.

As the reader gets into a book dealing with his concerns, he will discover that the author aims at opening up areas of inquiry for further reflection. Thus through what is being read that which needs to be said and spoken out loud may come to the surface in dialog with the counselor. In "working through" a given problem in this personal way, help may come.

WILLIAM E. HULME
General Editor

Contents

1. Pathways and Viewpoints — 1
2. Time to Change — 8
3. Courage to Grow — 15
4. Stresses in Family Life — 26
5. Hunger for Community — 38
6. Passport to a New Life — 48

1.

Pathways and Viewpoints

There are moments when we are brought up short by life and forced to take stock of ourselves. The shock of an unexpected event or the emergence of inner distress may make us doubt anything and everything—our work, our marriage, our place in the world, even the meaning of life itself. Then we find it impossible to go along in the same old business-as-usual way. We begin asking the really basic questions: Where have I been and where am I going? Is there any sense and direction to my life? What do I want most for myself and others? What should I be striving toward?

The occasions of questioning and doubt follow no standard timetable. For most, adolescence is a period of recurrent searching for values and goals. Often a critical decision about vocation or marriage raises far deeper issues, or the death of another may trigger a crisis of belief and confidence. For a great many, the middle years of life bring disturbing moments of unrest and reappraisal.

Sometimes it is difficult to define our discontent and disentangle its roots. When forty-two-year-old Durwood first went to a counselor, for example, he was not quite sure just what was bothering him. He was considered, and considered himself, a successful man, an advertising consultant with continuing contracts that included a major rubber company in a neighboring city. He was a devoted family man and had been an active worker in church and community affairs. Yet somehow all the zest and joy he once felt for life had vanished, leaving him only tired, frustrated, and irritable. He had begun to wonder whether anything was worthwhile anymore.

There were some specific problems he could point to, to be sure. He was overweight, and the doctor had cautioned him about rising blood pressure. He found the long weekly drive to the rubber company more and more exhausting, and had to fight sometimes just to stay awake. Yet his anxieties about flying prevented him from boarding an airplane. He worried about economic recession too, as the companies he advised began cutting back in the face of falling sales and production.

There was also trouble at home. He and his wife seemed to have drawn apart, arguing about small matters, doing fewer things together, losing the intimacy they once shared. She sometimes seemed so cold that he wondered if he were losing his sexual vitality and appeal. And he no longer seemed to have an easy companionship with his boys, who irritated him by neglecting homework and household chores.

Yet Durwood's problem was all of these and none of them at the same time. Taken singly or together, none of the difficulties would have seemed an unbearable burden at an earlier stage of his life. But now everything seemed, as he said, to be "getting to me." Now he felt unable to cope; as pressures mounted his inner resources declined. He sometimes wondered if there were any point to holding on to his career, his home, his faith. He felt trapped in midlife, and the more desperately he struggled the tighter were the tensions from which he wrestled to free himself.

Life was not all that bad, he was ready to admit, at least not all the time. He was satisfied with his work, yet dissatisfied with the strain and pressure of it. He was doing what he had wanted and prepared to do; yet caught in the middle of it he was frustrated and angry. He was striving to move ahead on the road to success, whatever the cost; yet he was beginning to wonder if the cost was too great. He hoped that his family would not disturb him with their questions and demands; yet he knew he was lonelier when they turned away and left him alone. He would have liked to believe in his wife and sons, his God and his world, or even himself; yet he was perplexed and undermined by doubts. What next? Where to turn now? Where was the course of life leading him, into what unknown future?

The problem for Durwood, and for most of us at a similar stage, was to reconsider his place in life in terms of a total self-understanding, and to regroup his forces to face the different demands of a new kind of future.

Dangerous Crossings

We in the middle years have lived long enough to know that life cannot be grasped all at once. We draw one breath at a time and take one step after another along one road that leads to another, and each event opens the way for all that will follow. We are constantly trying to remember where we have been and foresee where we are going next. Each person we meet calls forth a response and as we respond we become a part of all we meet, just as all persons and events enter into our growing experience of what life means. Life is a flowing stream that moves on a steady course, and to find the larger meaning of life we need to press forward toward the growing fulfillment of each successive stage in our journey.

Yet there are dangerous crossings in every life journey as we move from age to age. It is convenient to recognize the stages of growth as childhood, youth, and maturity. There are significant periods of growth within each of these broader landmarks. Each stage has its developmental tasks to achieve, such as learning to walk and talk in the early years of childhood. Each age has its particular crises, challenges, and frustrations to meet. Situations will differ, and yet in our society we have expectations for each stage of life by which to measure our growth and achievement.

The middle years may be defined in various ways. Here we will consider the years between thirty and sixty as our midlife. These are for many the most creative of all our years, when we reach the peak of our capacities and achievements.[1] Before thirty we

1. See Reuel L. Howe, *The Creative Years* (New York: Seabury Press, 1959).

are beginners, learners and initiators who are preparing to enter upon the major responsibilities of life. To a degree we must all remain youths, in the sense that we can never afford to stop learning or initiating no matter how long we live. We continue to have much to learn from those who are younger, just as we must absorb the learning and achievements of those who are older.

Crossing over to each new stage of life presents a crisis resulting from the new demands and expectations which we and others see as our responsibility at that point. Passing forty is often a time of inventory when we ask, "Have I arrived, or is there something else I must yet do before it is too late?" There is a sense of urgency: if I am ever to achieve my goals or be more creative I must be doing it now. And there may be forebodings of a vanishing youthfulness that betoken a critical turning point from ascending into descending life.

The approaching to fifty can be even more distressing. The menopause, for example, is often trying for the woman emotionally and physically. She is apt to see it as the end of her creativity as a woman, with declining beauty and personal attraction to others. She may resign herself in despair to "growing old" and being less alive, rejecting herself or fearing neglect from her husband. When children launch into career and marriage, the house may seem empty, the once exciting home drab and hollow.

The fifties are also difficult for the man in our society. Until that time he may view himself as a success, ascending the ladder of success in his vocation, gathering authority and power, sexually potent. Now he meets the crisis of yielding authority to younger persons, looking ahead to retirement, and moving out of a busy schedule where he was needed and wanted into the vacuum of no place in the world of productive work. What future can he anticipate? If he sits around home he may drive his wife to distraction or meet her resistance when he expects to have things his way. If he putters around the yard or goes out for golf or trailers, he may feel there is nothing useful or significant to fill his life with meaning. In a very real sense life may seem to be over, with nothing to do but to wait to die.

Actually, the crisis of aging may come at any moment when a person is aware of irreversible change. Trying harder to keep up with the strenuous pace, a person feels more tired and knows that he is slowing down. The aging process is more visible at times when the load seems heavier and the day too short or too long. There are hints and reminders, as we see in the mirror or in our contemporaries the telltale signs of aging. A profound and ominous sense comes to us of time running out and youth slipping through our fingers like the falling sand in the hourglass.

There comes a sense of looking downhill as if we had passed the crest and now must start along the steady downward course to the sunset of life. We may become aware of declining powers in sexual zest and potency, in physical stamina. There are slips of attention and memory; our keenness of mind fades. Health which once guaranteed vitality may dwindle or come to limits. A mood of ennui and distaste for the routine monotony of the day may settle like fine dust over everything, clouding the brightness of our vision. We may experience a painful sense of distance from other persons, especially the young. Looking for new adventures to strike out in the world of work or social life, we may see doors closing and possibilities narrowing with the advancing years.

Though the crises of midlife are common, we know that each person meets his situation differently in his own unique way according to his particular circumstances and characteristic style of life. What is true for me may not be true for you, at least not in the same way. Let us therefore see each person as unique, and focus on him as he really is, to see what he is trying to make of his life and how he can best grow through these middle years. They may be the best or the worst years, and only the individual himself can finally answer how to make them one and not the other.

Each person has his own journey to make, even though he will join with others. He is not identical with anyone, and he will experience life differently even within the same house or school, city or country. In fact, no two persons have exactly the same environment even though they travel the same streets and work in the same building. Within the inner meaning of life each person is unique and feels deeply the privacy of his own experience.

Yet we need to share our personal experiences with each other, lest we become lost in our private lives and separated or closed into a hidden world of intolerable loneliness. Rather than hiding our deepest feelings, we need to share them in open communication and mutual acceptance. Our best potential will be fulfilled only in concert with others.

To see clearly what life means to us in these middle years, we must be open with ourselves both to feel and to acknowledge our true condition. If we are open to our own feelings it is no longer necessary to hide, for we are willing to let others see what we truly are. This will permit us to explore our true condition in the presence of a counselor, or family, or friends and associates. Instead of expending most of our energy in holding up a brave front to cover our deficiencies, we can freely admit what we are and how we feel about life, to get on with the business of living and growing. This is most possible in a group or a relationship where we are mutually willing to accept each other. Then our contradictions and inner conflicts need not disturb us or trip us up in defensive efforts to conceal our misgivings and shortcomings. We are transparent to the light of truth and open to give and receive honest reports about ourselves.

While each person chooses the way his soul will journey, he learns from others and with others how to choose and how to travel through each day and the whole of life. In company with all we meet, we share life in every age with all ages and conditions of children and youth, and middle and late maturity.

The Road Ahead

Do I know where I am going? Where do you aim to be in the next ten or twenty years? How shall we find the road into the future we most truly seek?

Pathways and Viewpoints

As we meet in these pages our aim will be to see what we face in midlife. We come from widely different backgrounds in which each person is shaped by the social context in which he has lived, yet each of us chooses from moment to moment how he will respond to the changing scenes and persons around him. We are neither completely bound nor entirely free. Rather, we exercise freedom within the limits of this life in our world. Even as we are surrounded by difficulties we choose our own way to cope with the situation. And even as we choose the next step we move from where we were before toward new choices.

We will have much to learn from history and much to concern us in reviewing the events and experiences of the past. Yet after all is said and done, "What is past is prologue." What is most crucial is the present. And what is most decisive for our growth and fulfillment is a sense of the future toward which we bend the course of our life.

We shall therefore hope to keep our tenses in fair balance as we consider the journeys of midlife. Not to ignore the influence of the past, or to neglect the crucial decisions of the present, let us never forget that we are moving into the future. For the life we have in this present moment is always as fragmentary as the tick of a clock or the flicker of a pulse beat. It will not last, it does not contain its own meaning or purpose; that is found only in its impact on all the coming moments in our span of years.

To know each other we must meet with open eyes and hearty devotion. Let us search the beckoning goals that call us to leave the past for the greater future. Let us set aside the comfort of eternal rest for the adventure of dynamic and creative living.

In the next chapter we focus on the need to understand and welcome the fact of change. Change is everywhere inescapable. If we are to live and grow in a changing world we must accept change as the very stuff of our life. This is not easy, for resting in the established order of the past, rejoicing in the older ways is comfortable. Yet to meet the challenge of growth we must not shrink from but seize the fleeting moment to transform the living past into the enlarging future.

2.

Time to Change

Who Wants to Change?

We face a time of change. This is as true in my personal life as in the present stage of social life. Do I have to change? Yes—and right now with no delay. The whole world is changing, and whether we like it or not, we are changing too. Life is a process of continuous change. To live is either to grow or to decline, both of which are forms of change in one direction or another.

We are required to change, but we may refuse to accept it. Instead, we may resist and fight it as an unwelcome intruder into life as it was. It is easy to feel more secure and comfortable with the familiar. Here we have been at home, able to rest and rely upon the well-known context in which we have settled, where we are rooted, established, and natural. Not that life was ever quite perfect here, yet we have grown accustomed to it, and knowing what to expect we feel better able to put up with it.

It may seem that any change is hazardous in that it risks a turn for the worse rather than the better. Yet to fight change is even more hazardous in a world where other persons and the whole society is moving so rapidly that we may soon be as left out and irrelevant as the dead.

In the middle years of life, the responsibility to change is both critical and difficult. For we are growing older, and the process is visible for all to see. After what may have seemed an endless period to enjoy the exuberance of overbrimming energy and a confident feeling that we could do anything, we now become increas-

Time to Change

ingly aware of the load we carry and the fatigue growing heavier upon us. We are out of breath sooner, and though we press on, the strain is evident as the limits close in upon us. If change was welcome in the expanding years of growing strength, the new crisis of change is that it calls for larger withdrawals from our diminishing energy reserves. This we do not like or want to accept.

All around us we can see the "changers" and the "holders" taking sides. The changers call others to join them in transforming things and persons and society. They are the pioneers who launch expeditions to discover and develop new worlds. They are the social leaders who contend, like Moses with Pharaoh, to "let my people go." They are the scientists and inventors who develop new energies and resources for a larger life. They are the mystics who dream of wider horizons and the prophets who call us to claim the promised land.

The holders try to stop this process. They claim the old ways are the good ways and resist every change as an evil threatening the good life. It has always been this way, our fathers and mothers had it this way, let us be true to our tradition and faithful to the past. They call others to hold the line against newcomers, to preserve the status quo, to uphold what has been as sacred and untouchable, sanctified and unchangeable. They are the defenders of law and order, the upholders of the establishment, the protectors of vested interests, the powers that want to hold on to what they have and remain what they were.

Personal change in you and me is likewise a dynamic struggle between forces within that exert power to hold against power to change. Every person and family is a battleground in which the struggle goes on between life and death. Not only at the end of life, but actually in its very midst, the forces of decay are struggling against the forces of growth. Each of us, whether we like it or not, is engaged in this endless warfare of growing vs. holding on to what we have and are.

The struggle is particularly acute in the middle years of life. Ever since our youth we have sought to become established as a man or woman respected and secure. By midlife we have invested years of

Time to Change

labor in becoming what we are. We may have established a home, brought up a family, earned a position and a wage, joined a church, a labor union, social and political groups. We have invested so much in the established order, we belong to the world as it is. The people around us are our kind, and we dwell together in a sort of "peaceful coexistence." Never have we had so much to lose by change. We contemplate our losses as we feel our youth declining. We know we cannot hold on forever, yet we resist the changes that loom before us.

We who were once the masters of life are asked to yield our place to others. We must decrease that they may increase. This we know within our family as the growing young people approach and surpass us in strength, independence, and leadership. If we treat them forever as children, striving to hold the upper hand ourselves, we lose the battle and break up families into cold wars between bitter enemies.

We know how our forefathers sought to create wealth and master this new continent by taking the land from the Indians and by importing African slaves to toil on the land. This established a way of life based on mastery, with a master-slave economy. After a bloody war between the states the emancipation of slaves was declared. Yet the master-slave mentality has continued to afflict us as a plague. A century ago freedom was enacted, and now after a hundred years the Supreme Court ruled segregation unconstitutional, and asked the so-called masters to accept the once enslaved people in open schools with equal opportunity for growth as human persons. The change is painful and explosive. How can middle-aged white people who were once the masters accept black people as equals? Yet are we to deny children their right to learn and share life with us in one open society? Fear of change clutches the mind and rouses the passions to hold the color line and fight against change in blind fury.

We may wonder why there is this terrifying fear of social change, erupting into violence to defend the system of segregation. It is not easy to bear "the white man's burden," to uphold the myth of his supremacy, to be always vigilant to guard against constant danger of uprising or revolt of the oppressed and excluded. The master complex is a two-edged sword that cuts both ways, hanging over the heads of the oppressor and the oppressed alike. They who would master others will be mastered by others.

Whatever advantage in social prestige and economic power a master class holds is always in a precarious balance, never secure but subject to challenge and destruction because it is essentially indefensible. History has proved over and again that "uneasy lies the head that wears the crown." Only by force or deception can any person or class hold a superior position—and neither of these will last because they are never safe. How much better it is to accept all persons for what they are and what they contribute to our common life in one open community. Then trust may replace fear and panic yield to mutual sharing and serving, each for all and all for each.

When we come to the middle years of life, many of us are caught in some sort of master complex. For we have arrived at a position of authority in the family or leadership in the community. The goal of success is impelling in our society, and we are taught in every year of life to make good, to prove our worth by visible signs of achievement. In our families we urge each growing child to work harder, to rise to the top, to win over others, to keep up and get ahead of others. By midlife we have been deeply involved in this struggle to climb the ladder, be the top one on the totem pole.

Yet now we are pushed by the younger persons who are also striving for their place in the sun. How can we hold our upward mobility, and for how much longer, in this contest to ascend over others? Our mastery was heady wine that had the sweet taste of victory. But it is already dated, and will soon be outdated. We can see the handwriting on the wall and we fear the change that spells decline.

Freedom to Change

This brings us to a more searching question: How free are we to change? Can I really be otherwise than what I have always been?

Time to Change

Will you always be standing over me and against me to hold me in my place, or push me down to a lower rung on the ladder? If we have been conditioned by all the struggles of life to be competitors, how do we end the war and find a way to dwell in peace? No matter how much I want to change, am I caught in the tight vise of social pressures to hold me here like a trapped animal? Even if I try to change in midlife, to step down and yield room for others to step up, can I submit to you who once submitted to me? And if I have been the underdog, who will let me be the top dog without turning life into a dog fight? The time is upon us to consider how we will negotiate these changes, and where to go from here.

I believe we can find this the greatest time of life if we are willing to make it so. There will be losses to face, we can be sure; but there are discoveries open to us if we seek a greater life from here on. Not one frontier, but many frontiers are beckoning us to explore.

There are many dimensions of life to explore, each of which is calling us to new and exciting frontiers of change if we are to keep growing to enlarge the values open to us. Let us look at four of these dimensions to see the directions in which change may become growth. The ancient Chinese, who invented the compass, marked out *five* points—North, South, East, West, and Center. Our standpoint should be not from outside looking in, but from the center of life looking out. The center is where you and I stand as persons to observe the frontiers or horizons all around us.

The Christian cross is shaped to the form of man. Jesus on the cross stands for every man in his passionate suffering and courageous wrestling with the destiny of life and death. His feet point to the earth from which all life has risen to human form. His head looks up to heaven as the ultimate source and goal of creative purpose in fulfilling our highest being. His arms are stretched out to other men and women and children in self-giving love. Man is cruciform: the cross of suffering fits the basic dimensions of human life.

In the middle years, let us therefore suffer and give our best through each of these interacting and intersecting dimensions

Time to Change

which are open to growth. Along the horizontal outreach let me reach out to other persons from whom I have received so much. First I have known the family of my father, mother, brother, and sister who nourished me from birth. Then the family in midlife where I am husband to my wife, and father to our children, and grandfather to theirs. Once I received from these and countless others more than I gave. Now in midlife it is my privilege to give to others more than I have received, if that is ever possible. At least I resolve to major in giving that I may grow in the creative joy of learning anew that it is more blessed to give than to receive. Let me be strengthened by the awareness that every person I know is giving me more than I can realize, enriching my life with his contrasting moods and interests. This dimension we may call the interflowing and growing frontier of *interpersonal life*.

A second outreach is my response to group life in all its complex interrelationships. Let me care about my neighborhood, the community in which I live, the city, state, nation, and world of people. Here we meet the power structures that can cause injustice or promote justice, can reduce or increase the gaps between the ghetto of poverty and the suburb of wealth, the dark and the light, the haves and the have-nots. Is it not my privilege to participate in the society around me, and my responsibility to work for the freedom and dignity of all? Let me study the process of social change, and work with others for a better common life in which we share and care for one another in every condition. Midlife is a time to act with others in expanding the good society. This is the interflowing and growing *frontier of life in community*.

Along the vertical line of the cross, I look both upward and downward. Let me keep my eyes open in both directions. The head is reaching upward to discern the meaning of life and to find a purpose that is worth searching with all my mind and passion that I may fulfill my destiny as a responsible person. The center of me is a spirit seeking to know the potential greatness of life and to become more alive than ever before. In these middle years let me take this "insearch" more seriously, give more time and thought to inward growth toward that quality of mercy and wisdom that I have not yet attained. Let me be more truly religious in the center of my being, more ethical in my response to other persons, more patient in adversity, and more courageous to effect the needed change of growth in spirit. This is the interflowing and growing *spiritual frontier of life*.

A fourth dimension is our care for the body and the earth that is our home. Let me not decline into flabby inactivity but exercise vigorously to strengthen the body for later years. But let me not be obsessed with aches and pills and fear of illness and death. Rather, let me leap into the midst of life where other persons are in the swim of social action to create together a better community. Instead of preserving myself for my old age, let me give myself freely to sharing and working as a team. Let me talk when I need to with a counselor to explore my hangups and potentialities. Let me join a group that is growing and going somewhere, not killing time but using it. Let me enlist in a task force to achieve mutual discovery through service. Let me join the effort to create a better environment, reduce pollution of air and water, cherish the beauty of nature, restore depleted natural resources, and redeem the wastelands to bloom with new life in all the varieties and wonders of its vivid contrasts. This is the interflowing and growing *frontier of life in our world*.

Will you cling to the moorings of the past instead of venturing forth into the unknown future? On Cape Cod there are skeletons of old ships wrecked on reefs and shoals. There are idle craft standing by or rotting away while others sail forth. Carved in stone at the shore of Lewis Bay are the words of John F. Kennedy: "I believe this country should sail, and not lie still in the harbor."

We are bound to change, yes. But will we drift with the wind and the water, helpless victims of the waves and tides around us? We do not want to be beaten about and blown off-course like pieces of dead wood. We want to choose a destination, and shape that destiny which we will become. We will be buffeted and pushed and pulled this way and that. But with steady vision and all our powers, we can choose a course and decide how we will change.

3.

Courage to Grow

Dimensions of Growth

Let us take a new look at ourselves as growing persons. In what ways have I been growing through all the years since I was conceived in the womb? When these genes met in the microscopic cell, there was not much to me but a potential to grow. Yet as cells began to subdivide and multiply, there were wondrous changes through the nine months until I came forth a fully formed baby.

Instantly I was launched into a larger life-space of the family to live by relating to other persons, beginning with the doctor who severed the umbilical cord, tying the knot of my separation as an independent being. I was washed and clothed to rest in a crib until my mother was ready to nourish me at her breast.

One evening not long after, my mother was nursing me when there was a knock at the door. She opened it and saw a man standing in the moonlight, who asked, "May I come in and talk with you?"

She was startled to see a stranger at that time of night, when she was alone with two small children. Wondering who he was and what he wanted, she stood for a moment of indecision with the little son in her arms, and then responded, "Why yes, come in and have a chair here in the living room." When they were seated she could see he was struggling with conflicting emotions. Then he began to speak.

"I must tell you why I am here. I came to kill your husband. He ruined my business at the Seaside Hotel by asking the police to raid it and confiscate the liquor. I was standing behind the lilac bush at the corner of the house with a gun in my hand, waiting for him to come home from his evening meeting.

"Then I looked in the window and saw you nursing the new baby and rocking him to sleep. You were so beautiful and loving, my heart was moved. I began to think what it would mean to you and your little family if your husband was killed. So I came in to tell you I am not going to kill your husband."

My mother met her own challenge to grow that moonlight night. She was stung with sudden fear to hear this strong and agitated stranger say he had been going to kill her husband. Uncertain whether he might change his mind again, she wrestled with her impulses to flee or scream. She remembered that he was touched by her love for the infant son. Forcing herself to talk quietly with him, she came to accept him as a troubled person seeking a new way of life. She saw him change in her eyes from a desperate murderer to a person who cared for others.

When my father returned that night from a church meeting he was angry not only that his enemy had set a trap to ambush him but that he had invaded the sanctity of his home to talk to his wife when he was absent. But the more he listened to his wife, the more he realized that what had happened in his own home was a miracle of the unselfish love in which he believed and to which he had committed his life as a minister of the gospel. What amazing growth had come to this angry hotelkeeper, that he could change so profoundly in this crucial hour. And what courage his wife had shown to love this enemy at his moment of indecision.

The next morning my father went to see the man at his hotel and thanked him for talking with his wife so openly the evening before. He said he could understand how discouraging it was to lose that profitable business, and hoped he would make up his losses in other ways. The two adversaries began to understand and accept each other for the first time and in this reconciling mood my father invited him to come to church. He did come that Sunday evening, and again and again thereafter. Eventually he made a public confession that he wanted to be a faithful, working Christian and united with the church. By this time other members of the congregation who had once looked at him askance had begun welcoming him with growing affection and esteem.

The dimensions of human growth are almost infinite. What are the limits that you face as a growing person in a growing society of persons? The more we test the limits of what we think we can become, the more astonished we are. These boundaries before which we would halt our growth are not walls but open frontiers. What we find to our surprise is that our limits are mostly unreal obstacles set by ourselves or those around us as a final end of growth instead of an open challenge to grow anew.

Scientists from many fields are now converging on a very important discovery—the discovery of the human person. What they find is that most of us, whatever our age may be, are using only 5 or 10 percent of our human potential.[1] How can this be, when so many of us are working so hard to achieve, and straining so ardently to become more than we are?

Every person and every social group is in a process of growth or decline through the entire cycle of human life. Yet this growth is so often meager and faltering that it is usually minimal not maximal. We grow just enough to survive and make a "passing grade," to be comfortable and get by. In a world where so many are starving for food or hope in depressed areas and ghettos, there is a desperate struggle to meet the deficiency needs, with no surplus energy left for the effort to fulfill the growth needs of our larger potential.[2] *Potential* refers to the total capacities in every person which are not yet fully developed or used at the present time.

These are far beyond our recognition, yet within reach if we can learn how to release them. Some of these latent capacities are:

1. The potentiality for more effective and more satisfying relationships with other people.
2. Hidden or dormant abilities, talents, resources.

---

1. Herbert A. Otto, ed., *Explorations in Human Potential* (Springfield, Ill.: Charles C. Thomas, 1960); Gardner Murphy, *Human Potentialities* (New York: Basic Books, 1961); Jerome Kagan, ed., *Creativity and Learning* (Boston: Beacon Press, 1967).
2. Abraham H. Maslow, *Toward a Psychology of Being* (Princeton, N.J.: D. Van Nostrand, 1962).

3. The potentiality of increased creative productivity.

4. The capacity for exercising social concern and responsibility and for developing leadership in matters which affect the community.

5. The potentiality for a more vital, life-affirming existence.[3]

How do you and I intend to realize this vast human potential and develop the latent capacities so neglected within us?

Disciplines for Growth

A new awareness is dawning, after a long history of underestimating our potential, to be far greater than we are. We have been confined and restrained by many complex factors that impede our creative growth. A thorough study of these deterrents is urgent if we are to understand and tap the hidden resources of our human potential.

We need to look at our social institutions such as family, school, church, government, and the mores of our society to see how they may oppress our freedom to grow. There are social attitudes toward sexes, race prejudice, class prejudice, orientation toward work, toward aging, and token relationships that separate and alienate us from other persons. There are personal habits that retard and deprive us of creative growth through ingrained behavior patterns, dim life goals, lack of motivation, resistance to understanding oneself, and fear of risking ourselves in situations that invite basic change in our way of life.[4]

How do you discover your human potential and develop these hidden capacities? When I asked a physical scientist, Carl, he responded by tracing his life as a scientist to his present age of fifty. In the first twenty years his life was constricted in the depression era. His father was out of work from 1930 onward. "Severe privation has undoubtedly colored all my life. My sole ambition in the 1930s was to climb out of the financial morass." In the next decade scholarships and assistantships in college and university were a

---

3. Herbert A. Otto, *A Guide to Developing Your Potential* (Hollywood, Calif.: Wilshire Book Company, 1970), pp. 12–30.
4. Herbert A. Otto, *A Guide to Developing Your Potential*, pp. 39–129.

Courage to Grow

great help, and he gives credit to the professors who taught him true excellence, showed him patience by example, and opened many opportunities to him to become a scientist.

The next period (age 30-40) was a ceaseless struggle to establish a stable financial and professional life. His wife was interested in her own profession, and as soon as the children were in school she continued her Ph.D. work and career. "Although we were churchgoers, deep moral and ethical questions were not at that time much a part of my life. Life was a series of successes attained by tremendous effort." Carl continued:

After graduate study my career has spanned twenty years (age 30-50). The first years were spent in joining a profession, starting a life of research and publication and learning to teach. In those years being a scientist was an exalted calling. Participating in the development of nuclear energy, of aircraft turbine engines, of transistors and the like was exciting. Working in the defense of the country was considered to be noble. To be sure, many of us were concerned about what we were doing—I was a young participant in the debate on H-bomb development in the 1950s. But the patriotic fervor of the time overrode any objections we might have had.

Now in the 1970s scientists and engineers are thought to be despoilers by many of our population. This, in spite of the fact that most of us have been working toward making a more humane world. In fact, it seems somewhat ironic that the public which urged us on in 1950 in spite of our worries, should now brand us as being dangerous, if not evil.

These remarks are not intended to present a complaint or a picture of martyrdom. They are, rather, intended to portray an uneasiness, a questioning, a search for meaning in life. Some scientists and engineers feel it less than I, some a great deal more.

Carl speaks of one other man who shaped his life significantly. This is a minister whose church they have attended since 1951. He helped them through the loss of children and enlisted Carl in many positions of leadership in the church. Balancing the rather conservative outlook of this senior minister was a series of young assistants who brought a more radical, abrasive message which harassed, stung, and infuriated him. Yet he did not desert the church.

Angry and annoyed as I was, I could still see the sincerity and earnestness of these young people. At first ignoring them, then arguing with them and finally converging with them, I could gradually sympathize with and accept in some measure the views they presented. In short, they became a sensitizing agent, showing me a view of the blacks in the communities and of students in the multiversity previously not recognized. They are largely responsible for my entry into the governing structure of the university. There a number of like-minded people —administration and faculty—have changed this place and are continuing to do so. Whether it is fast enough, and far enough—who knows. We have done these things, however.

1. Developed a more realistic grading system.

2. Established one of the most successful honor programs in the country.

3. Enlarged the faculty governing body to include more low-rank members and some students.

4. Instituted the largest (I believe) special program for ghetto blacks of any residential university. Our 500 Program (i.e., a goal of 500 such freshmen per year) exceeds in size all the Ivy League schools combined.

5. Avoided serious trouble with unhappy students and faculty by seemingly endless talks and negotiations.

6. Increased curricular flexibility.

7. Modified disciplinary procedures to place more and more responsibility on students themselves.

8. Prevented repressive actions by legislature.

We can see how new and larger dimensions of growth have opened up to Carl as a responsible member of the university community. By this time he is a many-sided person of broader human concerns than the successful specialist he was in the early years of his profession. The church has deepened his concern for the blacks and the young people who seek to create social change toward a more humane and open society.

In addition to these efforts, another side of life was opened up through the church. When the senior minister left after twenty-seven years, a search committee which I chaired brought in a young man more to the liberal side. Supporting him during the difficult first year has been fraught with problems, but we embarked on the venture. He has showed me what true Christian caring is all about—first the mutual caring of a true community which is the congregation, and second the general concern for all men. Especially am I becoming ever more attuned to the plight of the ghetto Negro and unfortunate people everywhere.

As Carl charts the flow of his life beyond fifty he raises a question mark that shows how open the future appears to him. He knows that science is not the whole of life, much as he has learned through its disciplines. His life is outward-bound in new and broadening areas of human, ethical, and religious concern. Instead of narrowing down to a confining view and mode of existence, he is venturing forth to ever larger dimensions of service and devotion. He is unlikely to retreat into the private despair that often clouds the later years, but will, rather, press along new frontiers where human values are calling him forth to new adventure.

The Joy of Creative Life

Which of all your life experiences give you the most joy to remember? Those peak experiences are usually more than a pleasure of the moment or a sudden sense of relief in escaping a disaster. They are, rather, times of fulfillment and goodness when we have given our best, achieved some value, or met a crisis with courage. Such experiences remain with us as something we can approve and remember with *joy*. A truly joyous experience is not so easy to come by, and may often be mingled with pain; yet there is great joy in victory through struggle.

The birth of a child after strenuous labor may give a profound sense of joy, even when there are times of anxiety in the pregnancy, or distressing circumstances for an unwed mother, an impoverished family, an unstable marriage, or an unhappy outcome if the child is unwell or imperfect. Mary Jo recalls how the middle years are written large in both joy and pain. "We have found it remarkable how the more intense the pain the greater the potential joy. And we have slowly learned that our attitude—whether acceptance or rejection, hope or despair—has brought its own meaning to our life." She continued:

The discovery that our son Doug is mentally retarded was a disappointment of pain and almost despair. We felt the need for a faith, for we were unprepared for such a test.

The hold of pain on our life has never been entirely broken, but acceptance has come gradually, and forgiveness. It was more difficult to

Courage to Grow

accept the human imperfections that may have been involved in the birth of our imperfect son, and still more difficult to accept our own limited judgment and guilt in allowing such a thing to happen.

The redeeming feature was our decision to find whatever meaning there is in the disappointment, and not to use it as a source of defeat. Needless to say, his endearment to us in his good-natured response to life has brought comfort to assuage our grief. And not least, our experience with our son Doug has made us greatly more sensitive to the needs of others, both in and outside our family and church.

If we had these years to live over again, we would want to begin with the knowledge of ourselves that we have gained through these years of joy and pain. If we had known ourselves as we now know, if we had been as open and fearless in honest confrontation as we believe we are now, the joys we have known might have been even more abundant in proportion to pain.

In another century, pain was mingled with joy for Ludwig van Beethoven. He was a promising young piano virtuoso who was coming to be acclaimed as a composer too. When he knew he was going deaf, and could no longer hear music, he first tried to conceal his affliction, then gave up playing the piano in public, and kept aloof from all but his most intimate friends. In passionate protest he poured out his anguish in 1802:

> For me there can be no recreation in the society of my fellows, refined intercourse, mutual exchange of thought. I must live like an exile. . . .
>
> O Providence—grant me at last but one day of pure joy—it is so long since really joy echoed in my heart—O when—O when, O Divine One—shall I feel it again in the temple of nature and man—Never? No—O that would be too hard.[5]

Yet deafness sent Beethoven to composing music with a passion he had not known before. Removed from the society around him, he sought communion with the spirit. The solace of nature ministered to his bitter moods. Deaf to the sounds of music, he sought to capture the turbulent and majestic chords he heard within. A series of masterpieces came forth in rapid succession. After a decade of prodigious effort, he entered a period of quiescence. Then from 1818

---

5. Condensed from Milton Cross and David Ewen, *Encyclopedia of the Great Composers and Their Music* (Garden City, N.Y.: Doubleday & Co., 1953, 1962), pp. 50–54.

to 1824, the giant stirred again. Beethoven's later works were pervaded with a spiritual radiance that reached a climax in the "Hymn to Joy" of the Ninth Symphony. Here as never before his struggle with sorrow and adversity came to fruition in joy, and his vision of brotherhood of all mankind in a feeling of dedication to humanity.

In no other symphony had he voiced such an all-encompassing mood of humanity, spirituality, and exaltation. Without his affliction and the pain of his struggle to overcome it, there could never have been the joy of creative life rising as a fountain to overflow to others.

Awakening the Spirit

The greatness we seek is not far away. It does not lie at the end of a long journey to an unknown country. The quest for greatness has led man to pursue endless journeys in human history across every horizon from oceans to continents beyond, from earth to moon, from laboratories to the amazing energies locked within the atom. But to find the greatness of our human potential we need only to look within ourselves. To explore the intimations of this greatness is our next frontier where exciting adventures await us. The resources locked inside are actually greater than those locked in the atom. There is greatness dreaming within every person and society, if we can but awaken that dream.

Mark is a minister who has shared with me the inner side of his search for spiritual and vocational fulfillment. After ten years in the parish, he and his wife chose to pull up stakes and enter a Ph.D. program in psychology of religion in order to find a more effective way to minister to persons seeking a sense of fulfillment in day-to-day living. Mark writes:

I am the son of an obsessive compulsive perfectionist. To gain his favor I became a compulsive perfectionist. Performance was to be the primary concern. The yearning in me to be somebody worth loving drove me to perform well and to outperform all others if possible—in home chores, in school work, in athletic contests, in my vocation. Life for me was an agonizing struggle to measure up to presumed expectations of perfection in the hope of earning a warm response from those around me; and it was also a raging rebellion against the seeming injustice of such a demand. This inner conflict manifested itself in spotty performance, migraine headaches, and a rather joyless existence.

During my years in the Ph.D. program it began to dawn on me that the people I was serving as a student pastor were loving me—warmly, genuinely caring about me even when my performance was mediocre. A professor also introduced me to the meaning of "the gospel" through the Christian mystics, and there came a gradual awakening to the meaning of "grace." One experience during that time stands out. It was a week spent in an Episcopal monastery during a discipline of silence. There, "in community" with others contemplating the love of Jesus, I was grasped by a sense of what it feels like to be loved completely and unconditionally by the Creator and Sustainer of all that is. Yet it was a flicker of light, there one minute and gone the next, but unforgettable.

In the years immediately following, the need to perform in a new vocation confronted me also with the need to put performance in perspective. In a job, intelligence and skill are sold and bought for a price, and rightfully so, but I was gradually able to accept the fact that no one really expected perfection of me, and the cost of imperfection was not personal rejection.

My children also played their part in teaching me this. Mark, Jr., and Carol never stopped loving me despite the pressure and hurt I caused them by my perfectionist demands on them. Mark refused to perform despite great ability, and Carol kept trying even though her intense desire to measure up made it difficult to use the talent available to her. But it was I who was unloving, not them. Yet it was no easy step to accept them the way they were accepting me. I had to acknowledge and accept my own finitude instead of denying and fighting it, and to do it confessionally, openly, "publicly" admitting to them the errors and weaknesses in my own performance as a parent that were quite apparent anyway. But such openness "cleared the air" in our relationships, and we became friends. As friends we could openly accept each other as the warm, wonderful, bungling creatures we are. And that felt good to the very core of my being.

All along Jo Anne, and I had been struggling to find this same kind of mutuality in our relationship as husband and wife. This was complicated by the fact that we both inherited the same affliction. In our sensitive moments we had great empathy for each other, but in our insensitive moments each knew the deep hurt of rejection based on some failure to measure up to the impossible expectations of the other. Through such conflicts, however, we gradually lowered our expectations, gained a sense of humor, and came to appreciate each other more as we are: human!

Two factors contributed greatly to this: a sabbatical year, and our retreat in the Sierras. Both provided us with a chance for quiet reflection, and a chance to "claim" the love that was there all along. I had become so adept at rationalizing away the gracious concern of others that in some measure I had always lived as though it did not exist. When I began self-consciously to acknowledge and receive the love others offered, life took on a new perspective.

I know now that I am valued as *the person I am* completely apart from the work I do. So I work now out of a context of love, not out of a context of emptiness. Put in theological terms: having a continuing experience of salvation by grace, I am not compulsively driven to achieve salvation by works. As a result I have become a pastoral counselor with good news (a gospel) to share, no longer simply a psychological manipulator. I feel a genuine love for people where before I felt anxiety. I was afraid of people and angry because I was blaming them for making me afraid. Before, I was silent because of a lack of courage to risk exposure; now when I am silent I am listening to what others have to say.

Marriage is an increasingly richer experience of intimacy; we are at the same time more individual and more together, more unattached and more related, more involved in our own vocations and yet appreciative of the richness of our times together.

The greatest stress was in the agony of transition from a "Bad Father" to my son to a "Good Father"—adult related to another adult. Working through hangups in my relationship to my own father was hell, but I'm glad I made it with Mark, Jr. The greatest satisfaction emerged from the release of both children into adulthood, not only the continuing joy we experience in the relationship with them and their spouses and children, but especially the greater intimacy Jo Anne and I know in our relationship with each other. Looking toward retirement we have built a retreat house in the Sierras in which to continue a ministry to persons through small-group encounter.

In our search for greater fulfillment of hidden potential, we need to be free from the shackles that bind the inner spirit. This freedom we do not find alone but, rather, through relationship to other persons who offer a key to unlock the prison within. This grace to unlock our human potential is not far from any one of us. We begin the journey where we are. Yet we are never alone, because in this seeking of our spirit we find the answering Spirit creating us anew.

4.

Stresses in Family Life

Accenting Our Differences

When you have seen a family together you have probably noticed how much they look and act alike. The parents and children resemble each other in profile and family traits, in gait and gestures, in manner of speaking and behavior, and in attitudes. They are a unit interrelated by heredity and environment, by the sharing of life as an interacting social organism. We have long assumed that the cohesive family unit is the most important matrix of growing life in the shaping of character and human culture.

Yet within our own family many of us tend to accent our differences. We live so close together within the tight walls of home that each difference shows up in sharp contrast. When differences are exposed in the open interchange of family living, we stand out against each other in bold relief. "I am myself not you, and if you will see me as I truly am, my unique identity will come forth to confront yours." The better we know each other the more our contrasting ways are revealed and brought to the fore.

If we contend we should all be alike, we are asking for trouble. The individual is not and will not be the same as any other person. If you try to make me over in your image, I will resist with all my might your efforts to prevent my being my own person in my own way. If you see life one way and expect me always to agree, I will be determined to see it otherwise. If you offer me approval and love as rewards for conformity, I am tempted to be agreeable and fit into your pattern—but eventually I will need to assert my individuality as an independent person lest I become a mere shadow of you.

When growing young people are not invited to talk back, they act out their differences in subtle or vigorous ways. When we marry we try to please our partner and conform to his or her wishes and expectations. But when the honeymoon is over, we cannot long deny our unique individuality, which breaks forth in anger and love, affirming our need to be open with each other, to be known truly as we are, free to express our inmost feelings.

As our differences emerge we tend to play them up and contend over them. Which is better, your view or mine? Which is right, your way or mine? So we come to react increasingly to our differences and to treat them as sources of conflict. By one device or another we try to win out in the competitive game to gain a victory or private advantage over the other at any cost. Craftily we invent even subtler games to play up these differences and portray them in a manner to anger the other person and enjoy his discomfort. By digs "in good fun" or by sly needling we hurl darts dipped in sarcasm to release our own tensions and provoke a contest.

A well-known male gambit is to stereotype the other sex by repeating old saws and hanging crepe on the opponent in advance. "You know a woman has to have her own way." "She will surely have the last word." "Wives are always harping about something." "Beware of a mother-in-law, she is the worst thing about marriage."

Not to be outdone the woman has her poisoned barbs ready at hand. "What can you expect of a man, he is always late." "He never has time for his wife and children." "It's a man's world with no consideration for a woman's rights." "I know what he will say before I ask him." "He has no desire to listen or understand how I really feel." "Every time he opens his mouth he puts his foot in it."

In the same way we accent the differences between younger and older generations. The "generation gap" has been inflated to a major crisis in our society. "Never trust a person over thirty." "The old man is set in his ways, he can never change." "You can't teach an old dog new tricks." And from the other side, "Oh, you're too young to understand." "Look at that long hair, how crazy can you get?" "Keep away from those Hippies, none of them is any good." "You had better grow up and learn the facts of life." "Don't be so impatient for change."

So we teach ourselves and our children to mistrust one another. We type the other person as undesirable, or ridicule him and build a case against him as though he were an enemy. How strange, yet how natural, that we downgrade those we love the most until we ask if we love them at all. And how ironic it is to build a home and try to grow the best family we can while we undermine the foundation in these taunting, distorting ways.

Yet the game is enticing and private gains may lead us to risk the overall losses. If we play it shrewdly and gain the upper hand we have the advantage, enabling us to control the situation toward our goals. If we outplay the other, are we not proving that we deserve the rewards of success? If the other person is put in an inferior light, am I not showing my own superiority? In this competitive world, we say, each person will need to learn how to outdo the other person. Is it not good practice to win these games at home, especially if we are not winning our way so well in the larger world? When frustrations arise in the day's work, it is some release of tension to let go at home and transfer the hostility upon a more convenient target in the family.

As a matter of fact it is our differences as man and woman that joined us together in marriage. We are drawn to each other by the mutual and contrasting appeal of manhood and womanhood. It is by cherishing and admiring the distinctive qualities of each that we find the ecstasy of deepest love and the tender self-giving devotion that heals sorrow and distress. And between parents and children, is it not the very purpose of our living together to nourish growth in one another in all the variety of our individual differences? What could possibly bring more fulfillment to our life together than generously to give our unique personhood to one another, pooling our contrasting and complementary fragments to create a larger, dynamic, and interactive wholeness?

Let us be clear; incompatibility is not inevitable. It is not our differences that separate us, but the attitude we take toward them.

We are separated and set over against each other by attitudes of intolerance, irritation, anger, and resentment. When we exploit our differences to give hurt or gain an advantage, to prove the other person inferior and wrong, then we are demeaning his humanity and our own. When we distrust and decry another person solely because he is different, we make him our enemy and must prepare to attack or defend against him. Differences may draw us together in loving devotion or cut us apart in mutual hostility. By our attitude we may be either enriched or impoverished.

The Blight of Inner Separation

Laurie and Henry were married the summer after both graduated from the university. He was to enter medical school on a scholarship, while Laurie took a full-time job. They lived frugally until he launched forth into his career as a physician.

On the fifth anniversary of their wedding, they brought their first baby home from the hospital. Henry was in the midst of his comprehensive examinations, and Laurie had held her job as long as possible. But now their cup of happiness was brimming over; it flowed into Laurie's letter written at that time:

Oh, but she is lovely! Plump and strong, but daintily proportioned. I've been studying her dimples, but still can't decide which is the most fascinating. Her eyes are round and saucy, and at two weeks she learns how to roll them effectively.

Henry is the most adorable father I have ever seen. I watched "the parent look" dawn in his eyes one evening at the hospital when they brought the baby in for the ten o'clock feeding and he had his first long look at her—and he has been worshipful ever since. Sunday is his day for baby care, the complete routine from cod liver oil to the sun bath, and he wouldn't miss it for anything. His devotion is perfect. And as a husband he rates just as high! If he is as successful in his profession as he is in his family life, he will be a fortunate man indeed. But whether he succeeds in a worldly sense or not, I could never be richer than I am right now.

After the next baby came, however, the mood was different. Henry had changed greatly during his internship in another city, emerging a competent and admired professional man, and somewhat less interested in home life. Laurie was involved in helping her own family through a time of stress, in addition to baby care, managing a household, graduate study, and her job. They had grown apart during these few years. Just as they had come to the promised land toward which they had struggled and sacrificed, ready to claim the harvest of these years and enjoy the fruit of their labors, they saw that something essential to their happiness was missing. They had lost the deeper unity and intimacy of their married life. As Laurie poured out her grief, the loss was so great that nothing else seemed to matter. What could make up for this treasure of love?

I am losing Henry. And I love him desperately. This is the only disaster in life for which I have never been prepared. I am too numb to face the fact that I may have to live the remaining years of my life in a loveless relationship with a man who used to be my dearest friend in all the world. He is doing well in his practice and I am very proud of him. We have everything to make us happy but the essential magic of love.

Each of us can understand something of how Laurie must have felt in the pathos of such a loss. For she does not stand alone in that terrible emptiness. It may be that most of us at one time or another become suddenly or slowly aware of an inner separation from a person we have loved. Is there hope of renewing a fading love? How do we cope with moments of deepening separation?

Freedom to Love

Are we free to love? How do you respond to this question for yourself? Whether you say Yes or No, you probably would answer differently at another time. For it seems to me we are never entirely free; most of us might say, "No, not all the time" or "Not as much as I would like to be." Others might respond, "Yes, free in some ways" or "More free at one time than another." For life is complex, and as Shakespeare reminds us, "The course of true love never did run smooth."

Love is bound in more ways than we can mention, but some of the limitations are obvious.

1. We may be in bondage to the past by experiences in the first formative years of life, or by the conditioning of all our years of family living. Our upbringing may infuse our love with anxious or confident, repressive or releasing, punishing or rewarding, distrusting or trusting, sterile or creative, confining or expanding attitudes. Even our love for our parents may bind us to imitation of their constraining forms of giving and receiving love.

2. We may be bound to a future dream of instant satisfaction of all our desires, having our own way at any cost, impatient and inconsiderate of the desires of others. I may dream of such unrestrained freedom for myself that all else is tossed aside to enjoy my liberty. I may give such priority to the dream of success in a career that love of wife or husband becomes consciously or unconsciously an expendable matter.

3. Or we may bind our love by competitive patterns of living. The sibling rivalry of brothers and sisters can be extended into all relationships of life. Competition appears to be the dominant motif in our society. We study to excel over classmates and work to rise up the ladder to ever better positions, income, and status. We play and watch sports that glorify winning over rivals and receiving the trophies of victory. But the fierce game of competition distorts marriage and family, binding us to love of self and undermining love for others.

Where there is bondage there can be also the potentiality for release into a new freedom. Let us see how we bind ourselves, and how we may set ourselves free. A game is a series of transactions with other persons to gain some advantage. In family life we play these games over and over in interchanges that put others at a disadvantage and win for ourselves the contest. By such games we keep the other off balance—and avoid the intimacy of love.

Eric Berne notes that experiences of the past are so deeply recorded in each person that he may relive them as they are called forth by others in later life. We have a repertoire of three major roles or "ego states:" (1) the *child*, who continues within us and wants to be satisfied in the way we were—or wished we were—when we were a little boy or girl; (2) the *parent* who remains

Stresses in Family Life

within us to feel and behave the way one of our parents who was and is a dominant influence in our life would have; and (3) the *adult* who aims to appraise the situation objectively and make a reasonable decision.[1]

In life we alternate among the repertoire of these ego states, according to the situation and our personal needs. In the games we play, we may turn from one focus to another and call forth various moves from other persons in these transactions.[2] A transaction may be open and candid—adult to adult. Or it may be hiding an ulterior motive of gaining a private advantage. A transaction is complementary when appropriate and expected, as when a mother is nursing a sick child; each one fulfills the natural expectations of the other.

Tanjy, age 7, got a stomach-ache at the dinner table and asked to be excused for that reason. His parents suggested that he lie down for a while. His little brother Mike, age 3, then said, "I have a stomach-ache too," evidently angling for the same consideration. The father looked at him for a few seconds and then replied, "You don't want to play that game, do you?" Whereupon Mike burst out laughing and said, "No!"[3]

Children of course take naturally to games and enjoy them as much as parents. At the age of three Mike saw through his brother's game of stomachache, and responded to his father in the adult role of honest decision. At first the parents responded to Tanjy as a child and they played a child-parent game of an excuse to leave the table. But when the father responded to Mike as adult to adult, they both enjoyed the freedom to deal with the situation.

Games played at any age may seem frivolous, yet the hidden intent to gain an advantage can be crippling and self-defeating in the stresses of family life. A family game analyzed by Eric Berne as *Corner*, shows the manipulative barrier that is played to defeat loving intimacy. Here are the typical moves.

1. Eric Berne, *Games People Play* (New York: Grove Press, 1964).
2. A transaction is any unit of social intercourse.
3. Berne, *Games People Play*, p. 59.

Stresses in Family Life

1. Mrs. White suggests to her husband that they go to a movie. He agrees.
2. Mrs. White mentions that the house needs painting, an expensive job, when he had recently requested her not to ask for unusual expenditures at this time of financial strain. He responds rudely.
3. She says that if he is in one of his bad moods, she will not go to the movie with him, he had best go by himself.
4. Mr. White says if that is the way she feels about it, he will go alone, which he does, leaving her at home to nurse her injured feelings.[4]

In this game we see Mr. and Mrs. White each playing to doublecross the other and put him in a corner. There are two traps in which they can bind the other one. Mrs. White knows from past experience that she is not expected to take his annoyance seriously. What he really wants is for her to show loving appreciation of how hard he works to earn a living, and they will go off happily together. At the same time Mr. White knows that he is not supposed to take her pique seriously. What she wants is to be lovingly coaxed to go with him, but he springs his trap on her and she is left at home disappointed and resentful.

From a naive viewpoint, the winner's position is irreproachable, for all he has done is to take the other literally. But they both know they are cheating in refusing to play the game according to the rules of marital love. And the payoff is that there will probably be no sexual union when he comes home alone from the movie. Either one could have had it either way, but rather than to enjoy the intimacy of conjugal love, each one binds the other and defeats the desire for love.

When we bind ourselves in games to avoid love, we can find if we will a way to release the checkmate and be free to love. The choice is always ours, though the margin of consent may be slim at times. The temptation of gamesmanship is often strong enough to seem irresistible, and to drift with the momentum may be easier or more alluring. Our competitive maneuvers of defense and attack were not learned overnight. The double bind we put on each other has

4. Adapted from Berne, *Games People Play*, pp. 92–95.

been repeated over and over until we react automatically to every cue from the sparring partner.

The middle years will confront us with new problems. Yet we see that marriage partners are in a bind long before they come to the middle years. "Many middle-age problems are courtship problems, which because they have never been solved, mature in a final bitterness."[5] For life is a river in time, and while it may become deeper and calmer in places, it carries the force of its momentum and the debris of the past along its course.

Sensitive to Respond

To study the course of married love two social scientists of the University of Michigan interviewed 731 urban and suburban wives and 178 farm wives.[6] More than half of the wives were very satisfied with their marriages during the first two years; but twenty years later only 6 percent were satisfied, and 21 percent "conspicuously dissatisfied." Husband and wife talk less, interact less, and do less for and with each other in later years. The estrangement begins in the child-rearing years when the mother is overburdened with child-care and the husband is so engaged in his world beyond the home that he is inattentive. As the couple move into midlife they have been drifting apart for years. When the husband is insensitive to his wife's needs a wall of silence separates them, even as they live within the same home. When the children grow up and leave, and the house is empty, the wife often becomes bitter and depressed at the loss of her husband's affection and companionship.

If we are to enjoy the middle years we will need to launch ourselves upon a new life. Otherwise we live as strangers under the same roof, where life may be too lonely to endure, perhaps leading us to seek desperately for companionship elsewhere. Instead of creating a new life for these later years, "the revolt of the middle-aged man," according to the extensive observation of Edmund

---

5. James A. Peterson, *Married Love in the Middle Years* (New York: Association Press, 1968), p. 35.

6. Robert O. Blood, Jr., and Donald M. Wolfe, *Husbands and Wives: The Dynamics of Married Living* (New York: Free Press of Glencoe, 1960), p. 233.

Bergler,[7] is to fear the coming of age and to reject hi̶
the time of her own aging despair, while he frantically tr̶
capture his manhood in affairs with younger women, all to
Bergler's conclusion is that divorce won't help, but only
change within the man leading him to accept his age and find new
ways to give affection, so that he and his wife can share the harvest
of their years in mutual love and learning together. These are choices
only we can decide for ourselves.

John came home just four months after their last daughter had gone to college and found Jean crying. She had had high hopes for the time when their children had gone. She had always wanted to write, so enrolled in a writing class at the nearby college. She had many friends her age to be with, and she was going to take golf lessons one day a week. But she had too much time alone with no sound in the house, and there was a void in her life, until she became more and more depressed.

When John found her sobbing he took her in his arms and comforted her. Then he patiently asked her to tell him what was wrong and was able to understand. The next day he called the office and said he would not be in that day. It was springtime, and they drove out to a stream where the flowers were blooming. That week end he cancelled his golf game with his regular foursome, and instead took Jean to a driving range to practice. On Sunday they had a late breakfast, and spent the day talking and planning for the years to come. Jean's depression was gone.

It was not just the time together that was important. It was his understanding her feelings that helped most. It was his attitude that neither his work nor his friends were as important to him as she was, and this gave her the answer she needed. So she responded with deeper tenderness, and John discovered what he had missed during the years of their growing alienation. Together they planned each month to include more and more what they had both secretly wanted to do and share together.

Five steps forward seemed to account for a new spirit in their lives.

1. They achieved a new intimacy and tenderness.

2. They learned to intermingle their roles and share more of life together.

3. They developed a deeper relationship with friends.

---

7. Edmund Bergler, *The Revolt of the Middle-Aged Man* (New York: Hill & Wang, 1958).

4. They achieved a new relationship with their children.

5. They developed new and broader avenues of service in the community.[8]

John and Jean stand out in bold contrast to couples who meet the crisis of aging by turning their backs on each other in anger and despair. The middle years present a fork in the road. Some take one way and others choose another; some will relish and some curse their middle years. What a vast difference these choices make in the long road that stretches on into the future. Either we turn life into bitter hopelessness or we choose to enter a new life to find what we have missed before, and make these the best years.

Sharing Our Strengths

At one time or another it is likely that every married couple will find themselves in a rut. For marriage is a living organism that will pass through critical stages in its cycle. What once interested and satisfied us is no longer the vital center of our home. Then the questions may arise, Has our marriage failed? Shall we separate or, if not, will we bind ourselves to an empty round of dreary existence? Divorce may seem to be the threshold to a new life and many who go out that doorway hope to find a new mate with whom they can have a better marriage. But it is hazardous to run away from difficulties instead of working them through, for then they usually go along with us, and the outcome is often disappointing.

Those who go to a marriage counselor or perhaps join a group of couples in a Growth Center, may find open doors to self-awareness and mutual understanding within a marriage which had been at an impasse. Couples unprepared to wed in the first place and bogged down in the tangled thicket of marriage and parenthood may well learn new ways to develop their unrecognized creative potential through a loving family life.

When we enter marriage counseling or join a growth group, we are problem-centered, painfully aware of our defeats and failures, our irritations and frustrations. Each one has his gripes, ready to

8. Condensed from James A. Peterson, *Married Love in the Middle Years*, pp. 55–58.

Stresses in Family Life

blame the other for the misery at home, nursing his wounds in anger and bitter protest. We need first to hear each other out until we come to understand how the other feels, and to see how we can find better ways of fulfilling our mutual needs.

Then a new approach is needed that will enable us to share our strengths with each other and call forth the creative potential locked up in rigid defenses and routine habits of grim endurance. One marriage counselor invites husband and wife to focus upon the potential strengths that each one sees in the other, and to respond to them in hopeful expectation that each truly can nourish the other into creative fulfillment. He leads a group of married couples to search for "more joy" by discovering just what their present needs and desires are, and developing new styles of life to awaken creative joy in their life together.[9] This is a kind of "action research" in which both partners "invent" a new marriage, practicing new freedoms, actions, attitudes, and encouragements that lead to a giving and receiving of awakened vitality by mutual sharing of joys and interests, of larger purposes and a growing life.

Each of us suspects that we have been functioning at only a fraction of our creative potential. Loving responses can affirm and call forth this hidden potential through growing interest and faith in each other. Planned action and commitment can release this human potential in each member of the family. New family life must be a here-and-now, active, changing development not bound to the past. In the process, husband and wife will become aware of spiritual dimensions in their marriage, and give more room to develop resources of hope, faith, and love.[10]

If we are willing to grow there is an open threshold to a new life. And we will learn anew the truth of the saying, "Ask and you will receive." Give love, and love will be given to you.

---

9. Herbert A. Otto, *More Joy in Your Marriage* (New York: Hawthorn Books, 1969).
10. Herbert A. Otto, "Has Monogamy Failed?" *Saturday Review,* April 25, 1970, pp. 23–25, 62.

5.

Hunger for Community

Breakdown of Communication

As persons we have a persistent hunger for community. Solitary confinement is in some ways the most unbearable of all torture. Although we may often need to turn to solitude to find rest and relief from the pressures of social living, to pursue the inward search for personal identity, yet complete and prolonged isolation is so stifling and depriving that one is soon reduced to nonexistence —a living death.

A breakdown of communication with a person significant to you can sometimes bring you to the verge of frantic despair. Perhaps you have had such an experience as a child, as a young person, or even in later life. We may differ in our reactions to such a crisis —sometimes in anger and attack, in sullen withdrawal, or in grief and despair. There may be a feeling of helplessness and terror if we have failed in our best efforts to communicate; we may say, "It's just no use," and give up trying.

Each of us is nourished into personhood through our relationships with others. Whenever these interpersonal relations are disturbed we suffer loss and deprivations. Such losses come to every person at some time. How to restore and replenish sustaining and loving relationships that have gone awry is one of the most critical challenges of living.

Communication is the lifeblood of human relations, and when the interpersonal flow dwindles or ceases we become anemic and sick at heart. When dialogue stops, love dies and we are vulnerable to suspicion and hostility. But the renewal of dialogue can restore a dying relationship, bringing new health and wholeness to individuals and groups.[1]

To live in a family or a community without honest communication is too oppressive to endure. Hostility and prejudice poison the wells of good will, and existence is too bitter to nourish the human spirit. Without sharing of one another's feelings, without caring to bear one another's burdens, the walls of separation block the interflow of our life together. So community is no longer possible, and instead we dwell as strangers or as enemies.

The Anguish of Lonely Despair

Midlife may bring periods of emptiness and despair resulting from the loss or distortion of significant relationships. For many this will be the most typical crisis and difficult challenge of the middle years of life.

Erik Erikson[2] has charted our various developmental crises as a staircase on which we climb from one stage of life to the next. We cannot skip any of these upward steps or dodge the responsibility to work through the crises each age presents. These crises are psychosocial tasks which no one else can solve for us; because each person must work them through as best he can in the context of all his relationships.

The first crisis which the infant struggles with is *basic trust* vs. *distrust*. His whole future will be open if he learns to trust, or constricted if he is unable to trust.

The decisive issue for the young adult is to develop a personal identity as a man or woman, to know who he is, what he believes, and the nature of his vocation. This is the crisis of *identity* vs. *role confusion*.

In midlife we come to a major crisis of *integrity* vs. *despair*. In this time of life there are so many losses to face that it is natural

---

1. Reuel L. Howe, *The Miracle of Dialogue* (New York: Seabury Press, 1963), pp. 3–4.
2. Erik Erikson, *Identity and the Life Cycle* (New York: International Universities Press, 1959).

Hunger for Community

to despair. There will be separations from persons who are dear to us. Hope and aspiration will be undermined as we come to be aware that life is so limited and finite. We may feel ourselves reduced instead of enlarged. Illness or accident may curtail our freedom and vigor to enjoy all we would like to. Loss of position or income may deprive us of a security we had expected to last forever. Tragic events like wars and disasters, or injustice and social conflict may cause a mounting sense of futility.

To a sensitive person personal tragedy can sometimes seem like the end of the world. Cheryl tells of the crises that she faced in her struggle between integrity and despair.

Up until fifteen years ago, we lived as a fairly normal American family. Being in social work, we were not affluent, but we were happy. Then we moved from Wisconsin to Ohio, and from then until now we have literally lived through hell.

First, our sixteen-year-old daughter was stricken with schizophrenia. Shock treatments allowed her to finish high school and graduate as Valedictorian. She was a brilliant, talented girl, but after a semester and a half of college she was struck down again—and there followed eight nightmarish years in and out of hospitals. I will tell you one incident, when I learned the truth of what Dr. Viktor Frankl calls the "last inner freedom." Many nights our daughter was lost in the city —she would walk out of a progressive, open-door hospital. All we could do was sit, day and night; and hope and pray that no harm would come to her.

The last time the police called and said they had taken her to another hospital. We hurried out, and as I approached the door to Admissions, I saw her smiling face through the glass. A wave of relief went over me—she was all right. But in less than a moment, we had to realize that what we saw on her face was complete insanity. She could only make guttural sounds in her throat, and just as we had to leave, she fell to the floor in a convulsion. Her assigned doctor was ill, we had no friends or relatives—we stood alone that night. We drove home in silence, neither of us cried, nor did we cling to each other. That night I was certain of one thing—if we could live through this, the last inner freedom would never fail us.

She got well and is now happily married, with two lovely children. There is worry involved, but we must hope for the best.

Hunger for Community

In such a crisis we ask ourselves how any one of us would face a testing-time like this, when everything we had hoped for in someone we love seems to be shattered. We must find inner resources somehow to meet these crises of life. The inner freedom of which Viktor Frankl speaks was tested in the tragic experiences which he and his family suffered in the Nazi death camps.[3] Not only in his own testing, but from the vast number of experiences brought to him by his patients, Frankl discovered that the spirit can be free to rise above tragic circumstances if we will find a meaning by which to live, and a sense of unyielding purpose to make the best of whatever situation we are called to face.

One time of testing will be followed by others in the course of life. Yet the struggle to cope with each crisis prepares us the better to meet the next one, as we develop inner strength and freedom to affirm the power of the spirit over the gravitational pull of sorrow and tragedy. This fact Cheryl learned as she met her next family crisis with the strengths gained in her earlier struggle for integrity against despair.

Our second daughter was a beautiful talented girl who became a dedicated nurse—and she sang like an angel. When she married her high school sweetheart, home from Vietnam, I felt that at last she was safe and happy. She went to California where her husband was stationed. In a short time frightening telephone calls began to come from her. She begged us to come for her. Then came her first attempt at suicide. Even then we felt it was best to leave her in the care of her husband.

Then, a second attempt. She had punctured her liver and had to be operated on to learn the extent of the damage. She eluded the nurses and called me from the hospital. To my dying day, I will hear her voice across the miles, pleading for her father to come. It was the last time I was to hear it.

Before we could adjust ourselves to the horror of what was happening, her husband called to say that a judge had sentenced her as a criminal to a hospital three hundred miles from her husband (suicide is a criminal offense in California). As we were feverishly trying to find some solution, those men came—Lem's father and his minister. I

---

3. Viktor E. Frankl, *Man's Search for Meaning: An Introduction to Logotherapy* (New York: Washington Square Press, revised paperback, 1963).

thought they had come to comfort us—and then those words, "Fran is gone." I stupidly asked, "Gone where?"

Then I felt the impact of what he meant. I sat as if turned to stone. I could hear her sisters crying, and of all the foolish tears I have shed in my life—not one slipped down my face. Our darling was gone! Always and forever, we will have to live with that decision not to go to her. There were reasons, but they would not seem valid to anyone else —nor to us, now! If we had gone, she would be with us. I know that as surely as I am breathing. How do we live with a guilt like this? Sometimes it seems too much to bear, but we struggle up from dark despair, and seek once more to insulate ourselves against useless regret.

Two years ago I reached the end of my rope. In my extremity I called across the miles to one who had once been my friend, and he answered my desperate plea for help. Since that time exciting things have been happening. The first time I laughed, one daughter called to the other, "Come here, Mom is laughing." Sunday it came to a full cycle—I sang a hymn. Through love and acceptance my broken heart was healed.

In every loss there is sorrow. And often we are likely to be burdened with anger and the need to punish, or with guilt and regrets that lead us to reject ourselves. We may try to deny our grief with grim resolve or with forced gaiety—anything to repress the anguish and avoid the pain that shakes our souls. But the weight of these burdens can still rob us of all joy. Doubts eat away our faith, and hope gives way to the lengthening shadows of despair.

How do we come to accept loss and rise out of the quagmire that bogs us down in misery? We need first to pour out our grief in order to cleanse our pent-up feelings, and to talk freely with persons who care enough to listen to our deepest hurts and share the burden with us. If friends are near to listen and accept the outpouring of grief, we can experience a catharsis that opens the deepest wells of profound emotion. With a good listener we can relive the events that cause us so much pain, and so reduce their persistent power over us. Then we are more free to start a new life of openness and integrity.

Search for Community

The search for community reveals a profound human hunger. Basic needs are deficits, like empty holes to be filled. Until these deficiencies are filled, no one can be healthy or grow or fulfill himself as a creature or a person. A living organism has chemical needs, as for iodine or vitamin C, in order to attain bodily growth. There is evidence that love is just as essential to enable a person to grow. This is confirmed by the research findings of A. H. Maslow and other social scientists. Maslow distinguishes Deficiency motives from Growth motives. Deficiency motives seek to fill the basic needs for safety, belongingness, love, respect, and self-esteem, which are essential to a healthy person. The absence of love breeds illness, its presence prevents illness, and its restoration cures illness.[4]

Growth, in contrast to deficit hunger, is a fulfillment of our entire being in the largest possible sense. Such fulfillment is open to a person only in community with other persons. Wherever a true community of love, belonging, respect, and mutual esteem is open to us, we experience growth toward the actualizing of creative potential, spontaneity, and increasing acceptance of self and others. Growth in Being is not confined to any period of life, but may continue through all of life from the earlier to the later years. Older people, however, may suffer deprivations that shatter the sense of community and isolate them in lonely despair.

Love can have two directions that lead to opposite goals. D-love (deficiency love) is a hole to be filled, an emptiness into which love is poured. This is a deficiency disease, a love hunger like salt hunger, that is to be cured by making up the deficit. The person who does not have this deficiency does not need so much love so urgently, but only in steady, small, maintenance doses. He is well-enough supplied to uphold his vitality in the midst of strenuous living. And he is better able to withstand the shocks, recover from the losses, and meet the demands of life under difficult conditions.

B-love (being love) is love for the being of another person. It

4. Abraham H. Maslow, *Toward a Psychology of Being* (Princeton, N.J.: D. Van Nostrand, 1962), p. 20, 39–41.

Hunger for Community

is unselfish, unneeding love that overflows from inner resources and finds it more blessed to give than to receive. B-love is completely enjoyed without end, for it is nonpossessive and admiring rather than needing. D-love can be gratified, while B-love is not seeking gratification but self-giving. In B-love there is a minimum of anxiety and hostility. B-lovers are more independent, autonomous, less jealous or threatened, more altruistic, generous. B-love creates new life.[5]

How Do We Become a Community?

Many people live together in our cities, but few of them are neighbors to each others. Residing in the same street or apartment building, we do not really know each other. We have proximity without interpersonal relations. We live out our days and nights in narrow channels of life, going back and forth to work or market as strangers. We may recognize and even speak to the few who speak to us. But for the most part we walk and drive our city streets in a faceless and nameless crowd of unknowns. We are not drawn together by the sharing of our personal life. We note externals but we do not know the inner person. We act out our separate ways without interacting or transacting person to person.

A community is a group of people who know each other well enough to share life together. We are neighbors who belong to each other in the common interests and responsibilities of our life together. We care enough to listen to each other more deeply than in a passing greeting. We take the time and patience to let the other person speak of his real concerns, hopes, and distresses. If we truly accept each other we accept all of our faults and differences and eccentricities much as they amuse or bother us. If we want to know the other person we must put ourselves in his place, to see what he sees and feel what he feels. This becomes a costly self-giving of time, caring, helping, and sustaining one another in our joys and sorrows.

When Fred awakened he did not know where he was. He was in a large room with more than a dozen men dressed in overalls; some

---

5. In the language of the New Testament, D-love is eros or self-seeking love, while B-love is agape or self-giving love. See Anders Nygren, *Agape and Eros* (New York: Macmillan, 1939).

Hunger for Community

excited and noisy, others sullen and silent. Seeing others, dressed in white, he began to suspect he was in a strange hospital; and when he inquired of a fellow patient he learned that he was in a state mental hospital. Yet he had no memory of how he got there or what he was doing before he came. He was separated from every person and event he had known before. He was finally able to recall his name and some events of his earlier life, then his family, and his work as a college teacher and minister of a church. But all that was far removed from his present misery as a stranger in a strange world behind locked doors. This separation gave him a sense of hopeless despair, as a homeless refugee with nothing to call his own.

His first efforts to greet other patients failed, and silence followed every "Hello." Pehaps he had offended them or been so aloof they distrusted him. He decided to approach a group and ask what was going on. At first he was ignored until he said: "I don't know the score but am I a patient just like the rest of you?" They laughed and nodded sympathetically, while one said: "Good, so you're coming around at last. Damned if you're not a good Joe after all. You been bad off—way off your rocker." From then on he was accepted as one of a very exclusive club and began to feel a bit more at home.

Then came the Chaplain, who greeted him and asked how he was. When Fred asked about his family and how he got here, he was told that he had a nervous breakdown and had become seriously ill while preaching one Sunday. He was taken to a private mental hospital for two months and, not improving, he was brought to the state hospital for a series of insulin shock treatments to speed his recovery. At first only the nurse and doctor could see him. Letters came from his wife. When the time was right she came to visit him regularly, to bring him faithful love, letters from friends and news of the world out there.

The night before his wife came for the first visit he was sitting on the bed after supper, discouraged and weeping bitterly. He concluded he had been his own worst enemy, and "I have long been a stranger to myself." He felt he could never pray again, that God was too far away, and cruel to let him down like this.

Throughout the night he was reviewing his life more honestly than ever before. He confessed the long resentment for his father he had tried to hide, and the jealous rivalry he had all but concealed toward his brothers. Had he not acted out those feelings of resentment toward the church members who had disagreed with him? Had he not been striving all these years to prove himself and uphold his pride by success before others?

Confessing and praying to God in open and earnest repentance, there came at last the vivid sense that God was so near he would never again

Hunger for Community

be alone. "I could sense his compassion. Suddenly I felt no longer weary, exhausted, and wretched. His holiness overwhelmed me. And his understanding love comforted me."

That night was the turning point in Fred's recovery. The next day he was excited by the prospect of his wife's visit and to his surprise the entire ward was counting on it too. The news had spread by grapevine among his ward-mates. "What does she look like?" "Is she pretty?" "Is it true that she really loves you; and cares enough to visit you?" "What kind of a car does your wife drive?" With this information they look turns standing at the window for hours before she arrived. Fred himself was undergoing an inner battle of hope and fear.

Somehow as the door was unlocked for him to meet his wife he felt he was ready. They greeted each other with a kiss, not saying a word but just looking at each other. Then, "Fred it's wonderful to see you! I hear you're making splendid progress." They talked of the children, looked at the pictures and read the notes the children had sent. As she departed, smiling and happy, he had a new sense of confidence and self-respect.

His fellow patients were glad for him. "Boy, but your wife is beautiful." "She looks like an angel." "She acts like she really does care about you and believe in you." Others asked, "When is she coming again?" "Can we meet her next time?" Some of them were hurt because their family and friends did not write or visit them. They begged to read the letters from her, and were grateful when he shared them. They talked together of sex and religion and many other things in the long days they spent together. They came to know and trust each other in deepening friendship that continued after he was "graduated" from the hospital. Those who had come out and relapsed counseled him on how to cope with the dangers. Fred referred to them as "my little community."

He was heartened by many of his church people, who wrote him affectionate letters, had picnics for him on the hospital grounds, visited him, and awaited his return. When he did return in July with hopeful yet fearful anticipation, the church was filled. Before the service began several of the church leaders came to the church office to await silently and smile confidently. "Do they know that if they speak I might cry?" "And do they know what it means to me to have them come so glad to see me?"

Hunger for Community

Though he faltered in the early part of the service, he felt it was the deepest emotional experience of his life in public worship. "He is calling even a person like me to witness for him!" He preached on "A Light in Darkness." When the service was over the people lingered to give him a warm and loving welcome. Writing of this homecoming to his community who gave him faith, he says:

"I was deeply, but not tearfully, thrilled to meet them as their regular pastor again. I knew then that my emotions were profoundly healthy, genuine and normal. . . . God's grace was sufficient for me. . . . Happy and grateful beyond words, I felt that we had all done this together, with real teamwork and Christian kindness. I could not have done it alone—without my family, the congregation, and without God's understanding and mercy. Nor could we have done it without the moral support of my little community of hospital patients, and the expert guidance of the hospital staff."

His most severe test was yet to come when a determined minority who had opposed him before, now began a campaign of anonymous letters and telephone calls, urging him to resign. "You haven't got well yet, have you? Why be so stubborn?" "If you stay here you'll split the church wide open! Who wants to minister to a split church?" "A second crack-up will end you. You were a good college professor. Go back into education." "Getting sick again, aren't you? Your last lousy sermon proves it."

These encounters were strenuous but he sought to accept them in Christian love without striking back. They sent him to prayer where he faced them with God. "Forgive me for not loving these enemies as Jesus would have loved them. I know that their suffering is too deep for me to understand. O God, help me to remember that they are Your children, not mine, and that I am not their Judge and Redeemer, but You are."[6]

Wherever we are and whatever the circumstances, here and now is the best place and time to seek a community of life with other persons. If we have found joy in this life it is to be shared with others, who multiply our joy through their response. If we are to suffer anguish and tragic loss, we need to share our profound emotions with others who divide up our burden, and all are strengthened in bearing it together.

---

6. Frederick West tells the whole story in *Light Beyond Shadows* (New York: Macmillan, 1959).

6.

Passport to a New Life

Losses and Discoveries

Midlife is the time of greatest opportunity for the shared life and responsible work of our community. Others are depending on us for faithful service, and we must give up the careless freedom of youth in responding to the needs of those around us. We find fulfillment now in giving our best to others instead of turning away to seek our own ends. We give up one freedom and find a larger freedom in giving our life more freely for others. "He who is greatest among you shall be your servant" (Matt. 23:11). Giving up the freedom of youth we discover the greater meaning of life in creating a community of mutual response and loving service.

What we want most at this time of midlife is new discovery. We cannot go back to childhood to start over again and reshape the past to make it come out better today. Much of our daydreaming is an attempt to undo what we have done, going back to erase the mistakes of the past so that life will be different now. But to change life today we have to start here where we are now and find a better way into the future.

By this time in life we may shrink from the future because we fear growing older. The cult of youth in modern society leads many persons to see the age of forty as a final defeat of all their dreams of beauty and hopes of greatness. Yet there is a unique beauty for every age of life and, rather than hiding our age, is it not better to be what we are and enjoy the beauty of each age, to find the grace and dignity that is our true character? It is possible to achieve more creatively after forty, with the years of preparation behind us, and the opportunity to reach mature prespectives of meaning, of human understanding and wisdom.

It is surprising to find that many persons in midlife have a way of aging themselves by giving up a youthful spirit prematurely and secluding themselves from the growth and vitality around them. Herbert Otto describes this reaction against new life as "a negativistic attitude toward change."[1] Many maintain such resistance to change that they become old and out of touch with the world. By disapproving and rejecting all new styles of life and thought, new religious forms and social causes, they wall themselves into a prison to await impending death, away from the moods and modes of growth.

To be open to new life, we must take a basic attitude of interest and curiosity about the emerging styles of modern life. Instead of resisting or rejecting the new, we seek to understand and experience it more fully, to see how it came about and what it may contribute to personal growth and social progress. Such a readiness to learn will keep us growing in open relations to our world. And this will give a sense of wonder, eager anticipation, and thankfulness that we are part of growth and change.

What we truly seek is to discover a new life beginning with us right here and now. In the midst of our losses, we need to let go of the past no matter how inviting it may be, and discover a new life that is fitting to our age, promising new joy and fulfillment as we grow into the future. Paul knew this sense of expectancy: "All I can say is this: forgetting what is behind me, and reaching out for what lies ahead, I press towards the goal to win the prize which is God's call to the life above, in Christ Jesus" (Phil. 3: 13-14, NEB). When a tide turns, the change may at first be imperceptible. Yet the whole mighty current is moving in a new direction that is decisive for the future.

For many years David devoted his full energy to the practice of law in a growing city. He was deeply involved in court cases, lead-

---

1. Herbert A. Otto, *More Joy in Your Marriage* (New York: Hawthorn Books, 1969), p. 151.

...ecisions from the supreme court of the state. He
... in community activities, such as the Council of
... ic League, and political reform.

... ime he pursued a hobby in transplanting and grow-
... ies of roses, lilacs, and other beautifying shrubs. He
ca... bulletin from the Department of Agriculture on
domestica... g wild blueberries, and learned of work with blueberries at an experiment station. This so interested David and his wife that they began searching for a piece of land on which to develop blueberries.

When they began this work, near a lake in Michigan, it was a vacation project. Then as they became more and more interested in the blueberries, they sold their city house, and made their home on "Blueberry Lane," as they named it. Gradually, as the propagation and growing of blueberries required more time and attention, David reduced the days per week in the law office, to give more time to the developing of his new interests in a rural community. Eventually the new life surpassed the old, and they were deeply involved in a new full-time vocation. There was no open break from the past or sudden departure from one way of life to another. The tide turned subtly and they found themselves moving steadily and eagerly in a new direction.

Summing up their discovery of a new life, David says: "The peace and feeling of being near to nature was more fulfilling than the detail of law practice. I had had the thrill of court combat. Now I relish the quiet thrill of a new and beautiful azalea of my own breeding, or a blueberry of unique size and flavor. It is not a 'new life,' but the fulfillment at the ripening time of the old one. I wish everyone could have the same pleasure and satisfaction that has come with the idyllic happiness we have enjoyed in these forty-nine years we have shared together."

New Life for New Journeys

In the middle years it is clearer than ever that the former life is not going to be enough for the future. We have needed the struggles of growing up, the creative discoveries and disciplines in every age. Yet we now see that they are prerequisite courses to the

Passport to a New Life

more difficult and more inviting challenges that call us to keep on growing in the later years. Nothing that we have experienced will be lost or cast aside. For every road and every step of the way is preparation for new and greater journeys ahead. We can say with Robert Browning:

> The best is yet to be,
> The last of life, for which the first was made.

C. G. Jung knew how unprepared we are for the second half of life. "We cannot live in the afternoon of life according to the program of life's morning—for what was great in the morning will be little in the evening, and what in the morning was true will at evening become a lie."[2] In the first half of life, we are developing outreach, going forth to make good in the world, rear children, and care for others. But whoever carries over into the afternoon the aims of the morning must pay for it with damage to the soul. Then we need to search within to know life more deeply, to know our ultimate destiny to fulfill. Most of all, Jung concludes, we need to find a religious outlook on life.[3]

New life will be needed for unexpected journeys in the middle years of life. When June was happily married to Bob, she had no glimpse of a time in the future when they would be divorced. But when the time came and the long road of separation extended as far as she could see to the horizon, she began a new life and a new journey with her two sons. In this new road, she began where she was, yet she called upon whatever resources within her had developed through the years of living and suffering and growing.

As this year has turned from the time when Bob and I determined on a parting, there has been a gradual ripening of the joys of the new style of life. Yet I am sure beyond any doubt, that if I had known in advance that my wholehearted effort to become more mature would result in the ending of my relationship with Bob, I could not have mustered the courage to begin. For four years, at least, there was so much more pain than joy that I often wished I had not begun. But there

---

2. C. G. Jung, *Modern Man in Search of a Soul* (New York: Harcourt Brace and Co., 1933), p. 125.
3. Ibid., p. 264.

Passport to a New Life

can be no turning back of growth. Now I am beginning to enjoy much more than hurt.

I will try to tell you what I was developing inside me during the tough time, but it is hard to do, because the reality of it is nonverbal. The kind of "goals" I was developing are still not in words. The feeling I want to repeat and experience more and more is a kind of clean feeling. I have it when I have carried through a plan, especially one made with others, and seen the open, contented faces and appreciating looks that people share at moments like that. I also have it when I feel myself functioning naturally and well: physically (tennis, dancing, etc.), intellectually (inventing something or conversing), or emotionally (expressing feelings).

Patches of these good feelings have been growing into a way of life. Very often, and increasingly, with Bob I felt bafflement, and a sense of guilt and failure. I couldn't be what he wanted, and I couldn't imagine being good with anyone else if I couldn't be with him. He seemed some kind of an ultimate spouse. I am relieved not to have to try so hard any more. Being myself is much harder, because I have the whole responsibility for it and for my children too. But when I am doing well it's great.

My commitment to the family life goals that began before the first marriage is deepening in this period of single parenthood. I was disappointed with the boys' development two or three years ago, and had been for quite a while. Now I see how deep the fellowship between them is, and how patiently they are working toward a many-faceted fulfillment as adults. They astonish and delight me daily with their sensitivity, good sense, and resourcefulness. And non-sense! They wrestle, and they kid, and they try until they are exhausted to master some new skill. They dream, and they cry, and they shout, and they express their affection in very subtle ways. Our biggest disappointment as a family is in not being able to keep our head of the household really *with* us, but all three of us have increasing satisfaction in the life that is actually ours.

In this first year of separation she has been recovering from the agony of the four previous years. She has been at work as a librarian, trying to have some part in contributing to the growing life of inner-city children. Even with her long hours away from home, she has been able to accept her sons just as they are in this stage of growing up and to find a deepening relationship with them. She does not see her divorce as the end of the road but, rather, the launching forth into a new journey.

The End of Life?

Death has more power over us than we are ready to admit. Most of us fear death and try to look the other way to cover up the reality of it. Yet in the midst of this fearful awe that turns away from it, there is an uncanny fascination that draws us toward death. Where a man is poised to leap from a bridge or high building, crowds gather to watch his indecision, as if they too were asking, "Shall I live or die?" Death is a major theme in both daily news and great fiction and drama.

The mystery and challenge of death confront us ever more insistently as we come to the middle years of life. When those we love enter terminal illness and death, we know in our hearts we must somehow come to terms with the meaning of the end for ourselves. Is death the last great enemy? Or is it the great adventure of entering the doorway to a new life? Is it the end or the beginning?

Recently, a friend of ours was faced with a terminal illness. "You may have three months to live," the doctor said. How would you meet this crisis? For myself, I do not know how I would meet it. No two of us may respond in just the same way, yet we have much to learn from each other in how to meet death. We are, therefore, indebted to Laurel that she is willing to share her experience with us.

More than three and a half years ago, I was told I had cancer. There was no warning, no pain, just a slight tightening on my lower right side. I thought perhaps I had "pulled something" in attending a gym class the week before, or perhaps had "strained myself" lifting father in or out of bed. He was eighty-six years old, and had broken his leg three months before, and I was nursing him at home. In addition to the house and four children it was a heavy schedule, and I decided to check with the doctor; I couldn't afford a possible appendix at this point. (Little did I know what lay ahead!)

After the surgery, I think my first thought was disbelief. I had made Dr. John promise "not to pull any punches" about the outcome; I had always felt I could deal best with problems if I knew exactly what was involved, and I liked his straightforwardness in the past. Besides, I had decided this was a minor thing, and I was eager to get it over with, and bring my family together again. But the truth was staggering, as he described the seriousness of the situation, and the involvement of the cancer—over the entire abdominal cavity, covering most of the organs and upper respiratory area. No, they had not been able to remove it all, only tubes and ovaries, leaving the uterus—which amazingly was clean. I found myself consoling both my husband and Dr. John, who were visibly disturbed. Even then, I don't know how I knew, but I kept telling them both it would be all right. I had great faith in God, and a long and wonderful experience in relationship to him. He had never failed me (true, I had often failed him), but almost without thinking, and through force of habit, I knew I could trust him, and that everything would be all right.

But later, when I was alone, I faced myself and the situation and tried to take stock. Almost immediately came the question, *Why?* I am convinced now that everyone asks this question in a period of emotional crisis. It is as though our very beings know there *is* purpose in living, and, when confronted with the unexplainable, our souls cry out instinctively, demanding a just and rational reason *why* we should be asked to endure such experience. We implore meaning as though it were programmed into our souls by a Master Computer. As for me, I have come to believe there are no accidents. There is definite purpose in every crisis, and it is our responsibility to pause and find out what the purpose is.

But because I had long ago dedicated my whole life to God: I had graduated from a theological seminary; I was married to a Christian minister; I had reared our children in the Christian faith, and had continued to be as active as possible in church and as many church-related projects as I could—because of all this, surely I had a right to ask, Why? True, I had often asked God to *use me*. I wanted to be his instrument, wanted to help him fulfill his purposes in any way he chose to use me. *But not like this!* What possible good could be achieved in asking me, the mother of four children and much needed by a blind invalid, to die of cancer?

In the days that followed I received huge doses of drugs before leaving the hospital. Later, a maximum of X-Ray therapy. I lost all my hair. When I returned home, my sister came from Montana to nurse me through what I am sure we all thought were my last weeks of life. The house seemed empty, already dead, but I learned that solitariness was needed in order for me to come to terms with God. In the early hours in the hospital I had questioned his motives; yet I knew from the beginning there was *purpose* in all this, and there was only one way for me: to trust him completely, to turn over all doubts and fears concerning my family to him.

Passport to a New Life

In one respect I was extremely fortunate: I had no fear of death. I believe completely in life, and knew I would live, even though I died. *Christianity is resurrection*! Its most basic tenet is that man lives eternally. All of Jesus' life and teachings pointed in this direction. Two-thirds of the Gospel material is spent on the events of the last week of Jesus' life, and the entire New Testament is the story of twelve disciples crushed with despair and completely revitalized by the fact of the resurrection.

No, I was not concerned about death. It was my family, and what would happen to them. At this point my husband reminded me again and again of our beliefs, and together we examined our faith and re-evaluated every detail of what it was we claimed in our Christian experience. But this situation seemed too complex and serious to turn over to God and expect him to handle it. And so we tried alone at first to plan and organize our lives, and ignore the reality of death. But God is not to be ignored.

We have many friends. And about this time their love and concern and prayers began pouring in upon us in a way that was incredible. And this love and prayer changed our lives. We were reminded again and again by others what God can do, what he has done, and what he is doing. And we had to come back again and again to face him in our own prayers. We came to know again, as we had known almost from the beginning, that complete faith in him—absolute trust, and submission to his will—was the only route we could take. So we began to try. We did not pray for healing. (I never tell God what to do!) But we prayed for strength and understanding. We prayed that we might accept whatever it was he wanted us to do, and that we might have the strength to carry it out. We stopped trying to make long-range plans, and began living a day at a time. And each day we prayed for strength for one more day. The quiet and solitariness of our home during this time, without the children, enabled us to do this. In the weeks that followed, I held my own.

I continued to get well, and today I am completely well. Some said than what I can possibly supply them. If he allows me to continue on doesn't matter. I am functioning, and I have been restored to our family. If I need to go back into the hospital, I know now that God can handle that too. For we have come to know that our lives belong, not to us, but completely to him. He has entrusted us with a wonderful and fearful experience that has changed the lives of every member of our family, and many lives around us. And I know now that God's plans for the members of my family are better than anything I have planned, and his wisdom and guidance for their lives is far better than what I can possibly supply them. If he allows me to continue on with them, I will be grateful. I only know now that I would trust him in any circumstance, and I pray that if such a time comes again, I will not limit him by my own weakness, or doubt, or hesitancy. For we are his—and to the degree we accept his Will and Love in our lives, to that degree will his kingdom truly come.

Credentials of a New Life

If there is a new life open to us, why do we seem to miss it or make so little use of it? There is evidence to show that most of us develop only a small fraction of our full potential. And if this is true it is a tragic loss indeed.

How do we find new life and make the most of it? Is it the gift of years of living, or must we work for it? It is true that life is given to us with every breath of oxygen we breathe, with every ray of light and energy from the sun, every drink of water and nourishment. The cells of the body are self-renewing according to the organic balance of inflow and output of energy. Every person is stimulated and enriched by other persons, by interaction and communication in society. We are renewed and fulfilled by resources greater than our own. Every life is indebted to other life around it.

Yet we contribute to growing life, even as we receive from it. Regular exercise will increase our circulation and muscular capacities. A good rhythm of exercise and rest, of work and play, of sleep and waking, of quiet and activity will strengthen and steady the capacities to grow and maintain health and longevity. Spiritual resources may develop by the disciplines of regular practice, affirmation of meaning and purpose, and the utmost devotion to serve in outgoing love. The rewards of faithful growth are the fruit of labor and love. Insofar as we invest our growing powers we reap the riches of creative life.

What are the credentials of a new life? What passport will enable us to pass over from where we are to a new life?

The first credential of new life is *Be-ing*. To apply for a passport, I must be somebody. I must know who I am and identify myself to others. To identify myself I must know and be known as one who interacts with others. A human being is that being who con-

Passport to a New Life

tinues to be in the progressive present tense. In the continuity of his personal-social life he remembers the past and prepares for a future.

Other forms of life are renewing, but for man, to *be* is a rich mixture of complex and contrasting experiences.[4] To be a human being I must be born of human parents who give me a name and a home, a family cluster of interacting persons who awaken me, nourish me, and call me forth to participate in their life. They are concerned about me and I am concerned about them. What they do is important to me. What they think and say influences me. And reciprocally I am important to them. What I do and think and say makes a real difference and a vital contribution to their life.

When others recognize me as a person, I begin to recognize them as persons. Then we become a community of interdependent life, responsive to each other and releasing a renewing sense of freedom for each to be who he is. When the other identifies me and knows who I am, then I identify myself and know who I am. When we accept each other as unique persons who are significant in our own right, we give each other the "courage to be" who we are.[5]

This brings us to the second credential of new life, *Be-longing*. When we separate this key word into hyphenated syllables, the message can be analyzed and decoded into clearer and richer meaning. I "long" to "be" with you. I continue my "be-ing" by "be-longing."

Every person is a person in relation to other persons.[6] We belong together, and stand out ("ex-ist") only in contrast to and in community with each other. To *be* a person is to belong with other persons in a community of interacting life. Our communal life gives us our identifying passport as persons. To apply for a passport I must be authenticated by my country to enter another country, or to re-enter my own country again. The man without a coun-

---

4. See Rollo May, *Man's Search for Himself* (New York: W. W. Norton, 1953), and *Love and Will* (New York: W. W. Norton, 1969).

5. Paul Tillich, *The Courage to Be* (New Haven: Yale University Press, 1952).

6. Paul E. Johnson, *Person and Counselor* (Nashville: Abingdon Press, 1967); J. L. Moreno, *Who Shall Survive?* (Beacon, N.Y.: Beacon House, 1955).

Passport to a New Life

try is a lost and wandering ghost in a shadow world of faceless crowds where he is not known. A passport is the stamp of approval in which my country says, "Here is a person who is known to be a good member of our community—he belongs to us. If you respect us you will respect him."

By the time I come to the middle years I may be weary of my responsibilities to other persons not easy to live with. They expect so much of me, I have so much to live up to, I must measure up to what they demand of me, I may be tired of you and you and you, or all of you together. At this time of midlife, or even more at retirement, I may have a strong desire to "get lost," to go somewhere else, anywhere in fact, and the farther the better. Ah, let me daydream of far-away lands, where no one knows me, or expects anything of me: then I can start a new life, and be myself without interference of those who now "control" me.

But this is fantasy, deceptive and unreal. How can I go to any far-away land without a passport that authorizes me to enter as a person, one who belongs to other persons who claim me as their own? I can have recognition as a person in my own right only because you recognize me as one of you. To be myself I must belong to you, even though I may be tired of you. To "be" is to "be-long," and to extend myself through you. My life becomes longer and wider and higher because I am interrelated with you in a greater life. To belong to my community is to be more than I can ever become alone.

This brings us to the third credential of a new life, *Be-com-ing*. To apply for a passport I must come to you, my own country, and declare I belong to you. I will also declare that I want to go on a journey with your authority to admit me to other countries. As I come to the other country I present my *being* and *belonging* (who I am and with whom I belong as a member of my community). If these credentials are accepted my passport is stamped with the visa of the other country, giving me their authority to enter a new life there.

The "ing" in each of these credentials signifies the continuity of ongoing life, the sign of an active verb in the progressive present.

Here and now I am actively seeking to *become*. To "be-come" I must *be* a person who is becoming more than he was. If you are a "comer," you are not standing still or retreating in flight, but coming on to meet other persons face to face. To "come" is not flight away from a community of persons who weary me with the demands of our life together. Rather, if I come to you I step forward to meet you, I and Thou, in face-to-face encounter of intentional dialogue. I seek you in a new relationship we call meeting. Even if I have known you before, each time I come to you we are unique persons meeting to share ourselves and exchange life.[7]

"No man is an island," in John Donne's familiar words. "Every man is a part of the main, and whatever diminishes you diminishes me." For we as human be-ings share one mutually creative life in be-long-ing to each other. In these progressive steps forward we grow from be-ing a person, in be-long-ing to a community, through which we are be-com-ing a new and greater life together.

We have a friend who was born and orphaned on an island in the Caribbean. Many years ago he said to us, "I need a community." We responded: "So do we. Let us form a prayer group to meet and share our search for community." Through all these years we have lived our separate lives, each as a human be-ing moving on to his goals. Yet in regular group meetings we have shared our deepest joys and sorrows, our hopes and fears, our doubts and faith. We, though separate be-ings, choose a life of be-long-ing together. In sharing life so deeply we continue to grow into larger life in be-com-ing a community. Recently my friend put it this way:

> All my life I have wanted to live in a community of "caring" people. This was apparent to you when I asked our Prayer Group to become such a community. You were the kind of people on whom I could count to come to my rescue when my spirit was low, and the storm loud, and the night dark, and the soul was sad and the heart oppressed. I could depend upon you to bring me strength in my hour of need so that I could be secure within your love, until I learned to sing God's song alone in the night.

7. See Gordon W. Allport, *Becoming* (New Haven: Yale University Press, 1955), and *Personality and Social Encounter* (Boston: Beacon Press, 1960).

Passport to a New Life

Now I know that community is not self-serving; it is serving others. Here all around me is the whole community not only to help me, but also calling me personally by telephoning, and coming to my house, and writing me letters, asking me to help them when they are in trouble. Now for the first time I really understand the Master's words: "Even the son of man came not to be ministered unto but to minister, and to give his life a ransom for many." This revelation changed the emphasis of what I wanted, and has brought me my greatest blessing in life, first of all in spiritual matters, but just as much in the human sense.

To my surprise and great joy, I found that being concerned with and involved in the despairing needs of those around me, and those far off as well, I was no longer so afraid and anxious about my own problems and needs. In fact to my utter amazement, I find them being taken care of, so much so that even my greatest worry, one that has continually troubled me day and night for the past thirty-one years is now being solved to my satisfaction and blessing. I am at peace day and night.

Knowing my friend so well, I can see what a great change this is. He has found a new life far surpassing the old life when we first met. What better gift could we ask for in our middle years, and in all the continuing years than this? To outgrow the confining circle of self-centered living where I seek others to help me. To leave behind the outworn past for a journey not in flight from the old, but toward discovery of a new life greater than any we have known before. We seek to give life to others more than to receive it from them, to minister to others wherever they are. For we seek a greater community where other persons in need and lonely despair may with us find new being, belonging, becoming.

As we find this new life to give to others, even as we ourselves have received it, we become new creatures in a new and larger Being. Freely we have received from other persons more than we know or can ever repay. Our new life is more than a fountain of youth; it is a fountain of eternal life. And as we receive this fountain of life we are privileged to share it with other persons. The be-ing that reaches out to others in be-long-ing finds the joy of a self-giving community through which we are be-com-ing more alive than ever before. From day to day life is thus renewed through all the years flowing into eternity.